Sam the Star
and
Clown Fun!

By **Elizabeth Dale**

Illustrated by **Hannah Wood**

The Letter S

Trace the lower and upper case letter with a finger. Sound out the letter.

*Around,
around*

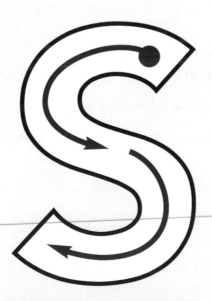

*Around,
around*

**Bolton
Council**

Please return/ renew this item
by the last date shown.
Books may also be renewed by
phone or the Internet.
Tel: 01204 332384
www.bolton.gov.uk/libraries

'Sam the Star' and 'Clown Fun!'
An original concept by Elizabeth Dale
© Elizabeth Dale

Illustrated by Hannah Wood

Published by MAVERICK ARTS PUBLISHING LTD
Studio 3A, City Business Centre, 6 Brighton Road,
Horsham, West Sussex, RH13 5BB
© Maverick Arts Publishing Limited July 2017
+44 (0)1403 256941

A CIP catalogue record for this book is available at the British Library.

ISBN 978-1-84886-288-3

www.maverickbooks.co.uk

This book is rated as: Red Band (Guided Reading)
This story is decodable at Letters and Sounds Phase 2.

Some words to familiarise:

show   dance   trick

High-frequency words:

the   a   I   as   he   is   of

Tips for Reading 'Sam the Star'

- Practise the words listed above before reading the story.

- If the reader struggles with any of the other words, ask them to look for sounds they know in the word. Encourage them to sound out the words and help them read the words if necessary.

- After reading the story, ask the reader why Sam was the star of the show.

Fun Activity

Show each other your craziest dance moves.

Sam the Star

The sheep do a show.

The sheep sing well
but Sam cannot.

The sheep do tricks,
but Sam cannot.

The sheep jump well
but Sam cannot.

Sam is sad.

He cannot jump, sing
and do tricks.

Do a dance, Sam!

Sam **can** dance well!

The Letter C

Trace the lower and upper case letter with a finger. Sound out the letter.

Around

Around

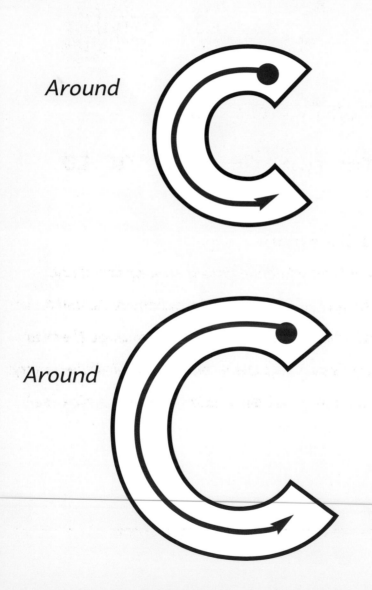

Some words to familiarise:

clown   flower   bucket

High-frequency words:

is a the has he it in at to

Tips for Reading 'Clown Fun!'

- Practise the words listed above before reading the story.

- If the reader struggles with any of the other words, ask them to look for sounds they know in the word. Encourage them to sound out the words and help them read the words if necessary.

- After reading the story, ask the reader what made Max feel better.

Fun Activity

Ask the reader what else could appear in a circus.

Clown Fun!

Max is a clown for the day.

Beppo has a pie.

Beppo throws the pie. Splat!

Max has a pie.

Max throws the pie.

Splat! Bob is mad.

Bob has a bucket.

He throws the bucket...

But Max is not wet!

Bob has a flower.

The flower has water in it.
Bob squirts it at Max.

Book Bands for Guided Reading

The Institute of Education book banding system is a scale of colours that reflects the various levels of reading difficulty. The bands are assigned by taking into account the content, the language style, the layout and phonics.

Maverick Early Readers are a bright, attractive range of books covering the pink to purple bands. All of these books have been book banded for guided reading to the industry standard and edited by a leading educational consultant.

For more titles visit:
www.maverickbooks.co.uk/early-readers

 Pink

 Red

 Yellow

 Blue

 Green

 Orange

 Turquoise

 Purple

 Book Band Red

Dog in a Dress and Run, Tom, Run!	978-1-84886-290-6
Buzz and Jump! Jump!	978-1-84886-250-0
Bam-Boo and I Wish	978-1-84886-251-7
Sam the Star and Clown Fun!	978-1-84886-288-3
Seeds and Stuck in the Tree	978-1-84886-289-0